SUNKEN TREASURES

STORY BY: J. LEW
ILLUSTRATED BY: MISHA

Copyright © 2017 by J. Lew

Sunken Treasures
By J. Lew

Printed in United States of America

ISBN 9781946806031

All rights reserved solely by the author. No part of this book may be reproduced or transmitted in any form or by any means without the written permission from the author.

www.jlew-books.com

A Chris Adventure Book

J. Lew

Chris, Toni, and Danny are excited. Today their parents are taking them to the pet store to purchase an aquarium, and fill it with beautiful fish and their favorite accessories. Chris loves the diver, Toni prefers the mermaid, and Danny has his eye on the pirate ship.

"Mom," Chris calls. "Can I have the diver? I'll call him Toby."

"I want the mermaid," Toni says.

"Can we please get the pirate ship?" asks Danny.

"You can each pick one thing," says their mother. "It's not a very large aquarium."

"This will be so fun," Toni says. Chris and Danny agree as they bound into the store.

The basket is filling up fast. All three kids have picked out what they want for the aquarium. They are now shopping for Candie, their poodle.

"She needs another chew rope," says Toni. "Her old one is all worn out."

"And she needs more of those bacon treats," adds Danny. "We're running low on those."

"They already thought of everything," shrugs Chris. "What can I get her?"

"How about a new collar?" his mom suggests.

"Okay," Chris says happily. "Let's get her a blue one — blue is my favorite color. Now everybody has something!"

They check out at the register and leave the store.

Everyone is beaming. They pack up all the parts for the aquarium themselves.

"I'm strong because I can carry two boxes and Toby all by myself," announces Chris.

"I'll put all the boxes in the van because I know how to stack them, and still leave room for the aquarium and Candie's treats and toys," Toni says.

"I'll be a helper too," interjects Danny. "I can carry boxes, and help put them in the van."

After their dad puts the aquarium in the van, they all climb in, put their seatbelts on, and begin their drive home.

"I can't wait to get home and show Candie our new aquarium," says Chris.

"Us either," agree Toni and Danny.

They are all smiles the whole trip home.

Chris, Toni, and Danny can't wait to put their pieces in the aquarium. They have already picked out the spots where they will place them.

"The ship is the most important thing in the aquarium," says Danny.

"No, it isn't," Toni disagrees.

"Mine is more important than yours," says Chris.

"All the pieces are very important," their dad says. "The ship is important because it holds the pirate's treasures."

"Told you," bragged Danny.

"Well, Danny, the mermaid is important too," adds their dad. "She knows where all the treasures are."

Toni sticks her tongue out at Danny.

"And finally, the diver is important because he finds all the treasures," he explains. "They all play an important role in the aquarium."

Filling the aquarium is taking longer than Chris expected. He sits on the couch with Toby, waiting for his dad to finish assembling the aquarium, and falls asleep. Chris dreams he is the captain of a pirate ship with his first mate Toby.

"Hurry up, me mates, we have to shove off and be on our way," says Captain Chris.

The men are bringing lots of boxes and chests aboard for their voyage at sea.

"Make ready the sails, Mr. Toby," the captain orders. "We shove off as soon as the last man is on deck."

"Aye aye, Captain," says Toby.

Captain Chris and his men are ready to set sail, and find more treasures of the deep.

Captain Chris and his crew are sailing the high seas. Toby spots some friendly dolphins swimming alongside the ship.

"Ahoy, Captain!" Toby calls. "There are dolphins on our starboard bow."

"This is a good voyage," the captain says. "Our friends the dolphins will lead the way."

"How many are there, Captain?" asks Toby.

"Count with us me, mate… one, two, three, four, five, six. There are six friendly dolphins playing in the waves."

When you are on a ship and need directions, you will hear phrases like *port side*, *starboard side*, *stern*, and *bow* when you are facing forward. The port side is the left side, the starboard side is the right side, the stern is the back of the ship, and the bow is the front of the ship.

"Wow," says Captain Chris says to his crew. "I know you will be great shipmates."

So where are the friendly dolphins swimming alongside the ship? That's right — on the front right side.

Chris and his mates have boarded a small boat used for diving and retrieving sunken treasures.

"All ready, Captain?" asks Toby.

"Ready." Captain Chris gives a thumbs-up.

He and his mates are ready to dive and search for the pirates' treasure.

Captain Chris has made many dives into the oceans of the world. He loves to swim along the reefs and observe the many different sea creatures that live there. What kind of sea creatures do you see?

Captain Chris says, "You should be very careful not to pick up a jellyfish when you see it on the beach, or even when it's in the water. They can sting you with their long tentacles."

He continues to swim, and asks, "Did you know the coral on the reef are living sea creatures? If you snorkel, or visit a large aquarium, you will see live coral. Make sure to ask the attendant what they eat."

Captain Chris swims on as he searches for the treasures of the deep.

"Whoa," says Captain Chris. "I can't search that sunken submarine for treasures because that giant octopus has made it his home.

"How many tentacles or arms do you think an octopus has?" he asks.

Here's a clue — count to seven and add one more.

"Did you know that an octopus has three hearts?" he asks. "Two of its hearts pump blood through its two gills, while the third pumps blood through its body. Wow! That is a lot of hearts."

Captain Chris can't stop now. He is mesmerized, and swims past the octopus and its home.

"I can't believe it!" says Captain Chris. "I'm flying! I'm flying just like the stingray."

Stingrays flap their sides like wings. This helps them to soar across the ocean floor.

"Some stingrays have teeth that allow them to crush their food like clams, oysters, and mussels," he says.

Then Captain Chris's expression grows serious. "You must be careful with most stingrays because they have a barb under their tail. It is very dangerous, and they use it for protection."

Captain Chris continues to flap his arms like the stingray while he searches for treasure.

"Now that is a real under-the-sea treasure!" exclaims Captain Chris. "It is a big, shiny pearl inside a giant clam."

Two eels swim out from the rocks and stay next to the giant clam and its treasured pearl.

Giant clams are real. So if you're going scuba diving, you'll find them on the reef or in the sand, but you will have to look really hard. You see, they blend right in with the reef!

Eels can be dangerous because they have strong jaws with very sharp teeth. Those teeth help them hold on to their food.

Did you know that eels have two jaws? The eel's second jaw is behind its head, tucked right in its throat.

"Wow," says Captain Chris. "I'd better keep going."

Captain Chris swims away from the reef and into deeper waters. There he sees an anchor with a mermaid. The mermaid points to the many treasures of the sea.

"In this ship you will find many treasures," the mermaid informs Captain Chris. "But you will have to search the ship to find them. Make sure to keep watch, because sharks love to swim in sunken ships."

There are many sunken ships around the world, and many captains who search the seven seas far and wide for those ships. But few are found with golden treasures.

"Thank you," says Captain Chris.

He will swim to the ship and search it for the pirates' treasure.

Captain Chris stands on the deck of the ship and gazes at the ocean's sandy floor.

"This is amazing," he says. "This place is just like dry land — it has valleys, mountains, and deep canyons."

Then he remembers the mermaid's warning.

"Oh, no," says Captain Chris. "I must hide!"

Captain Chris must swim away fast. He sees a big shark heading his way!

Can you spot where Captain Chris is hiding?

I knew you would find him! He's hiding in the hole inside the ship.

Did you know that a shark can lose more than thirty thousand teeth in its lifetime? That is quite a lot of teeth. Captain Chris knows that he must be careful and keep an eye out for sharks.

Humans lose all of their baby teeth by their thirteenth birthday. That means we lose twenty teeth before we are thirteen years old. By age twenty-one, we have thirty-two permanent teeth.

"Keep brushing your teeth and gums," says Captain Chris. "Brushing helps to keep our teeth strong and healthy."

"That was a big shark," says Captain Chris.

After the shark swims away, Captain Chris is safe to search the ship for treasures.

He exhales a sigh of relief and swims to the cannon deck. There he finds cannons and cannonballs — great treasures for the museum.

Captains used cannons to protect their ships from pirates, and could be found when ships went to battle at sea.

Captain Chris will have his trusted shipmates dive to the sunken ship and bring these cannons and cannonballs aboard, to be placed in a museum for all to see.

"This must be the captain's cabin," says Captain Chris. "There's a chest by the table."

He opens the treasure chest and finds nothing inside. "I thought for sure it would be in here," he says.

There is something in the room that will lead Captain Chris to more treasures on land. What do you think it is? Did you say the treasure map on the table?

"Great job, mate!" says Captain Chris.

This room has many treasures for the museum.

The pirates' flag with the skull and crossbones is known as the "Jolly Roger." Pirates often flew a different flag to fool other ships until they were close enough to attack, and then the captain would give the order, "Hoist the Jolly Roger." By then it was too late for the other captain, and he would have to surrender his ship and its treasures.

In the corner of the room, Captain Chris sees a pirate protecting his treasure. It's Captain Red Shirt, sitting in his favorite chair.

"I sure hope this chest is full of treasures," says Captain Chris.

When he tries to open the chest, he discovers it is locked. "This must be the real treasure chest," he says. "I'll have to send it to the ship and open it on deck."

Captain Chris puts the treasure map, the flag, and both swords in the empty chest.

Pirates did not always bury their treasure. In fact, they spent most of it on the islands where they lived. Many of the pirates lived in the Caribbean. Some lived on the island of Nassau, Bahamas.

Do you remember where the two swords are?

That's right! One is hanging above the map on the wall, and the other is in Captain Red Shirt's hand.

Captain Chris has a lot of work to do. He must send all the treasures to the surface where his shipmates are waiting.

Airbags are often used to float treasures from the ocean floor to the surface. These special devices are called Lifting Bags. They make things easy because sunken treasures can be very heavy. Men and women at sea fill these bags with air, much like filling a balloon.

Now that Captain Chris has found the ship's treasures, his mates will dive too and collect all the other items for the museum.

"Well done, Captain Chris," say his shipmates. "You have found the sunken treasures of Captain Red Shirt.

"Thank you," Captain Chris says modestly. "Now it's time to dive back down to the ship and recover all the other treasures."

"Aye aye, Captain Chris — we'll make ready for the dive," say his mates.

Captain Chris will watch from his ship as his shipmates send up the cannons, the cannonballs, and the chest from Captain Red Shirt's cabin.

Captain Chris and his first mate are congratulated and rewarded for finding the sunken treasures of the deep. He has offered the treasures to the curator of the museum for everyone to see.

"Thanks to Captain Chris, we now have the sunken treasures of the pirate Captain Red Shirt," the curator announces as he shakes the captain's hand.

"Thank you, Mr. Curator," says Captain Chris. "I know there are more treasures to find, and I will do my best to recover them."

Toby, his first mate, waves at the cameras.

A curator is responsible for keeping all the treasures in the museum.

When you visit a museum, you get to see things from the past and from all over the world. There are treasures of all kinds from land, sea, and even outer space.

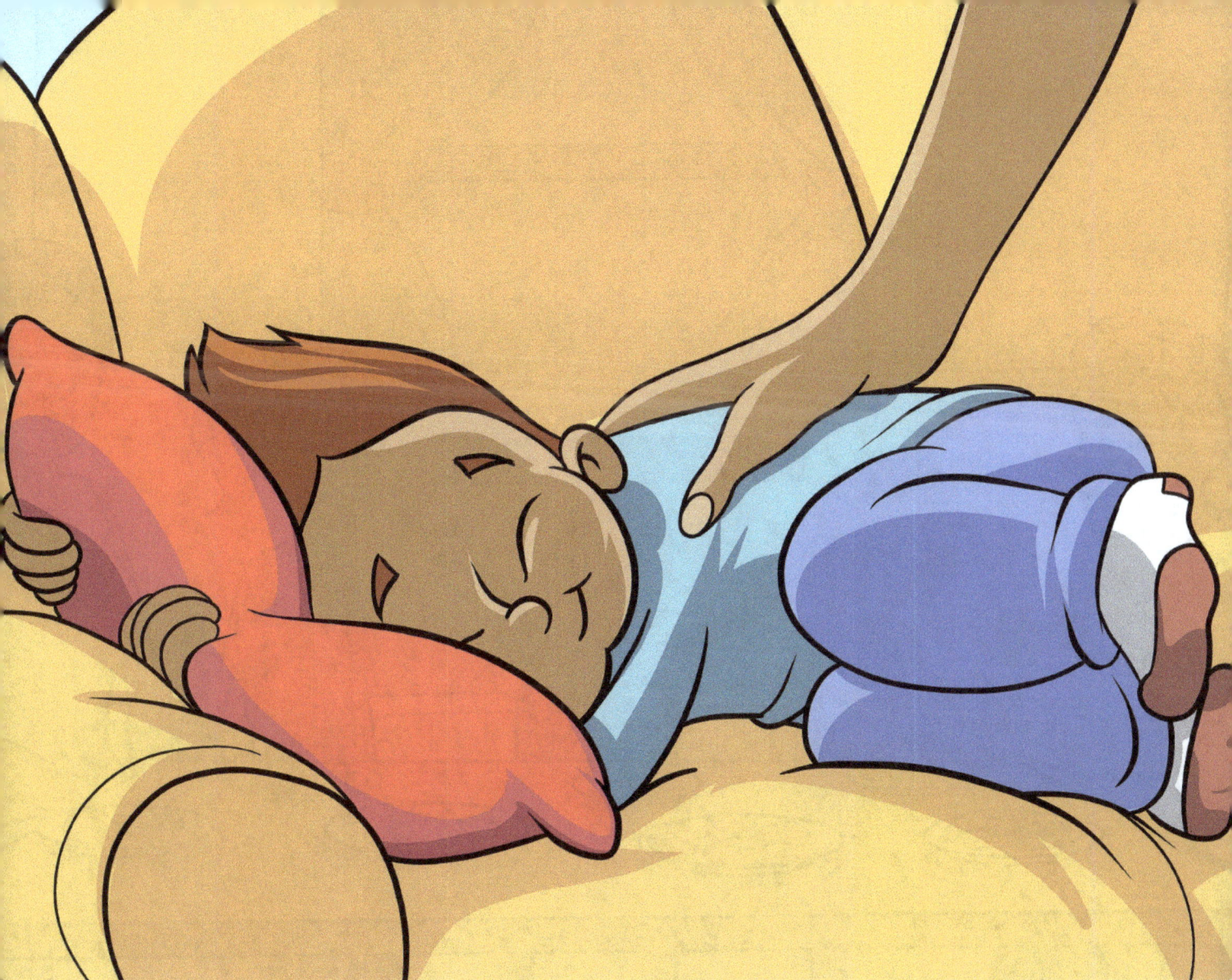

Chris is still asleep on the couch when his mother wakes him and tells him it is time for dinner.

"Chris!" his mother calls. "Wake up."

Chris yawns and stretches. "Is the aquarium finished yet?" he asks.

"Yes, it is," his mother replies. "But you must wash your hands and eat before you look."

Happily, Chris washes his hands and sits at the table. He can't wait to tell his family the incredible story of the sunken treasure.

At the table, Chris hardly eats a thing. He can't wait to share his adventure under the sea.

"Chris, you have to eat your food and then tell us the rest of your story," says his mother.

"Sure, Mom," he replies. "But I didn't tell you about the big shark circling the ship."

"Were there a lot of treasures on the ship, Chris?" Toni asks encouragingly.

"There was gold, and a crown, and…"

"Chris," his mother says firmly. "Please eat your food."

"Ah, but I just started my story," Chris pouts.

"We'll finish your story later, Chris, okay?" says his Dad.

"Okay," Chris obeys, and eats all of his food.

When Chris has finished eating, he is allowed to see the aquarium. He has to stand on a step stool to gaze at all the wonders inside.

"You see, Toby," Chris says, "our diver is really important. He swims in the sea and finds the treasures to exhibit in the museum."

Chris is proud that his diver is the one of the most important pieces in the new aquarium. He pictures himself as the diver, still searching for more sunken treasures in the sea.

SUNKEN TREASURES

A Chris Adventure Book

More books by J. Lew
I'm Not Afraid of the Dark

Coming soon are more of Chris Adventure books!
Little Ranch Hand
Chris's Family Vacation at Rocket World
A Day at the Doctors

J. Lew

www.ingramcontent.com/pod-product-compliance
Lightning Source LLC
Chambersburg PA
CBHW081400080526
44588CB00016B/2554